a spiritual guide for the
UNEMPLOYED

a spiritual guide for the
UNEMPLOYED

TIMOTHY MULLNER, DMIN

Liguori

ONE LIGUORI DRIVE
LIGUORI MO 63057-9999

Imprimi Potest:
Harry Grile, CSsR, Provincial
Denver Province, The Redemptorists

Published by Liguori Publications
Liguori, Missouri 63057

To order, call 800-325-9521, or visit liguori.org

Library of Congress Cataloging-in-Publication Data

Mullner, Timothy.
  A spiritual guide for the unemployed / Timothy Mullner.—1st ed.
     p. cm.
  ISBN 978-0-7648-2060-1
  1. Unemployed—Religious life. I. Title.
  BV4596.U53M85 2011
  248.8'8—dc22

                              2011016035

Liguori Publications, a nonprofit corporation, is an apostolate of the Redemptorists. To learn more about the Redemptorists, visit Redemptorists.com.

Printed in the United States of America
15 14 13 12 11 / 5 4 3 2 1
First Edition

To Carol and Ken.
Thanks for housing the homeless.

CONTENTS

FOREWORD

One of the deep principles underlying our contemporary way of life is the principle of pragmatism: What has value is what works! But pragmatism has a nasty underside; its reverse also appears true: What doesn't work isn't of value. We live in a culture that, for the most part, values us for what we do, rather than for who we are. For the most part, our self-image is inadvertently formed on that basis. When we are doing something useful, we feel useful. When we aren't achieving something, we feel useless.

To lose a job brings much more than the worry and anxiety of paying bills, meeting mortgage payments, and supporting a family. Unemployment is, first and foremost, a crushing blow to our self-image. The additional side effects of job loss can bring humiliation before our family and friends, an experience of being cast aside by colleagues, a forced exile from where the action is in our profession, or exclusion from the work relationships we may have developed at our job. All of these "symptoms" can cause a painful tear in the very fabric of our sense of self-worth.

When we find ourselves unemployed, the deeper questions are not: "How do I pay my bills? How will I pay my mortgage?" These are worrisome questions; however, they are not our deepest pain. We know we most likely will not starve. More deeply, we question, "Who am I? What does my life mean if I can't work? Am I of value?" The powerful stigma attached to unemployment can affect even the healthiest pride. Because unemployment is so humbling and painful, the deep blow it brings to self-esteem is not immediately recognized. The wound is noticed only later in unanticipated anger or depression as the humiliation, too painful to admit, seeps out anyway.

As I read Timothy Mullner's *A Spiritual Guide for the Unemployed*, two phrases kept coming to mind: A symptom suffers most when it doesn't know its identity. And: Not everything can be fixed or cured, but it should be named properly. Using a mixture of poetry and prose, Timothy Mullner names well what happens to us when we find ourselves unemployed. As a physician of the soul, he skillfully connects our symptoms to their real root. Beyond that, he offers valuable prescriptions to help turn the pain of humiliation into renewed personal depth and peace of soul. *A Spiritual Guide for the Unemployed* is a valuable and much-needed book.

RONALD ROLHEISER, OMI

INTRODUCTION

Unemployment wasn't at the top of my bucket list, but on June 27, 2009, I joined the 15+ million Americans who were unemployed or underemployed.

After five years with a Fortune 500 company, my position was eliminated. I had terminated staff before. It was a painful process as a manager and terrifying for employees. Now it was my turn.

In a culture where the number of zeros in a bank account brings status and identity, I was left with my family, my faith, a bunch of degrees, and a lot of experience. Without my VP title, staff, and expense account—who was I? And where was God calling me on my journey of faith? I was about to find out.

Thanks for taking this adventure with me. I hope these stories, prayers, and reflections will help guide your own experience. This isn't a book to be read and put away. Take some time with each chapter. Throughout the text I emphasize certain words or ideas through capitalization, punctuation, or lack of punctuation. As you read the book, imagine that we are having a conversation through the text.

Also, by noticing what's happening within and around you, a pattern may emerge, or a new path might present itself. Start a Reflection or Journal folder on your computer for your entries. Better yet, grab a pen, a notebook, or a bound journal and write your thoughts and feelings as you sense the "tug" of the Holy Spirit.

While you are looking for work, remember you are NOT your job. You were created in the image and likeness of God (*imago dei*) and you are *very good* (Genesis 1:31). Your value comes from WHO you are, not only what you DO!

Be willing to explore fresh options and open new doors as you reflect on your gifts, strengths, and skills.

Never forget your inherent dignity as a human person. Your understanding of the real value of your work can make this period of unemployment a time of discernment and hope, as well as personal and professional growth.

May these challenging days of waiting, job hunting, and longing for reconnection lead you to inner peace. They did for me.

TIMOTHY MULLNER, DMIN

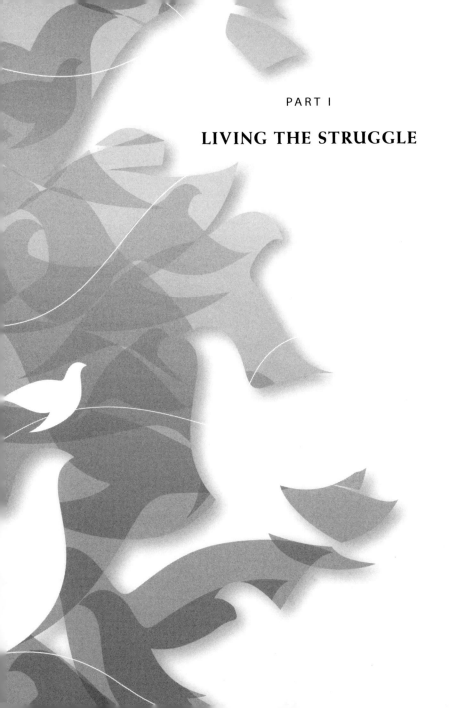

PART I

LIVING THE STRUGGLE

CHAPTER 1

HEARING THE NEWS

Oh Lord, I've been pushed off a cliff.
I am falling—and fast.
My heart is racing, aching for peace.
Hear my prayer, O God. Stop this free fall
With your healing hand.

Amen

Accidents and unemployment happen. Are we ever really prepared for either one? But it's different when you lose a job. There are no obvious broken bones—it's all inside...How do you repair an entire life—or a lifestyle for that matter? What do you do first? Especially when all you want is to go back to how things were before?

The root of the word "obey" means "to hear." And that's the only choice I had...Except I couldn't hear anything—just a rushing sound in my ears. There was no discussion, no other option. No one asked what I thought about the decision to terminate me. All I could do was obey... And I had to do it quickly—and most of all—quietly.

Does that sound like how you felt? Large job or small—downsizing, layoff, or restructuring. All you can do is obey and leave. Clear out your office, close any accounts, empty your desk, and hand over your keys. "Hand over my keys??" Wait—How will I get back in? Oh, that's right... I'm not coming back in.

Part of obeying is listening. It's hard when you feel like you have just been punched in the gut—but try...Try to hear what is really going on with your emotions and your thoughts, even while life as you knew it is whirling around you. Are you BREATHING? The most common response to stress and trauma is to hold your breath. So stop it! Take a deep breath—Yes—right now. IN and out. Slowly...in and OUT. And again—No—really try it—now repeat...

So are you breathing? Was leaving such a bad thing? Are you sad, or in shock, or numb? Or do you feel relief? The key is not to avoid reality—it will still be there when you get back! Wade through the pain and allow these prayers to be a mental, emotional, and spiritual "life jacket." You are not alone. The Spirit of God is as close to you as your very life-breath. You also have family and friends—and people you haven't even met yet—for support. If you don't think you have anyone—try to reach out and ASK for support! If you can't, it's OK...

So don't panic and be sure and congratulate yourself—You picked up this book! Now slooowww down and listen to what's going on in your life—pay attention to your deepest, truest inner self. This is your time to listen, to hear, and to obey the Lord's call. God only knows what will happen next!

A New Beginning...

My world came crashing down
Not in a violent fashion
but over the phone

My intuition was on "high alert" Lord
The memo the day before
was all I needed to clean my office
rearrange my desk
and create room for the news

It was not good. At least at first

The phone rang and my heart was still
Mind-racing, heart percolating, no fear

The voice on the other end
delivered the news of separation
Carefully positioned
to cover the HR-legal angles

A "Termination and Release Agreement" is coming
Who agrees to be terminated?
How does one release 5 years, 1,825 days, Lord?

How do you measure 5 years in a life? In...
sales orders or monthly reports?
In airline miles, lost luggage, or hotel points?
In company car miles and time away from family?

My world came crashing down Lord...

I hung up the phone
with initial numbness
yet the presence of mind to breathe deeeeep

And then it came. Out of nowhere
A prayer from deep in my heart and soul
Words came without thought or created syntax

My first syllables were "Thank you, God!"
For what?
For being fired?
For the coming "Termination and Release Agreement?"

No. "Thank you, God!"
I had a choice…
Via negativa—the negative way
or *via positiva*
And my soul had spoken

It was the path of grace
The choice of joy and hope
in the midst of pain, hurt, and loss

My world came crashing down Lord…

But I was not really hurt, Lord.
In fact I was being healed
Pushed out, forced by the Spirit
to follow my passion, my hopes, my dreams

Now my life is being rebuilt
One day at a time
One phone call at a time
One breath and one dream at a time

Lord, I feel like a movement from chaos
to *kairos*—a holy time—is taking place
Time directed by You and Your grace
It is Spirit-given time to pause
catch my breath, and welcome a new vision

My world is being reconstructed Lord
Holy order is the order of the day...
Tugging me toward wholeness
and real inner peace

My world came crashing down...
and I did not go to pieces, Lord

Thank You for this "Surprise" ending
and new beginning

Amen

Fare Thee Well

The final meeting
   was awkward and quiet
We covered the agenda
   with dutiful somberness
We all felt it
   but couldn't speak the words

Letting go is hard, Lord
   when colleagues become friends
And the future
   isn't very clear

How do I say
   I'm sorry for this ending
   I wish you the best?

Lord, thanks for Your presence
   in this uncomfortable
   process of letting go

Saying Goodbye

"So long, I wish you the best"
"I will miss you"
"Let's keep in touch, OK?"

Letting go is hard, Lord
It's difficult to open my hands
    and my heart
    to move on

Help me to be gracious,
    yes, full of grace
    as I depart

Lord, make this ending
    a truly "good" bye
    a fond farewell

Give me the courage,
    to not look back
    and carry no regret

It is good to move on
    with You at my side
    into the by and by

Confidentiality

Lord, there's so much I want to say
but can't.
It's always a plus when colleagues
become friends.

But now my hands, no my lips
are tied.
The agreement says I do my job until
the end.

Then, and only then can I reconnect with
    lost colleagues
    old friends
    dear souls
    and celebrate!

For now I need to keep it
    tucked inside
    in that quiet place only
    You see

Thank you for knowing my
        deepest thoughts
            heartfelt desires
            and hopes
                for peace.

Can we keep this between us for now?

The journey toward healing and hope is not always easy. You have chosen to open yourself to God's grace and the "tug" of the Holy Spirit. Your emotions may be raw from leaving your company or even a job that you hated.

The following questions may help you feel—or at least think about what's going on inside of you. Writing can be a way to discover what you are thinking or feeling—about anything.

So, grab a notebook or go out and buy a beautiful writing book to begin your new adventure! Take some time to think about these questions. Answer them in your head or write down your thoughts. Then put it away for a while—But, be sure and come back—to listen and read about what's going on in your mind and heart. Then—open your soul to God and prepare for what comes next...

For Reflection

1. List the emotions you experienced or what you thought about as you left your job. How did you feel when you heard the news? Write it down.

2. Who was the first person you told about losing your job? What was it like? What do you remember most? What would you tell that person now?

3. What Bible verses, memories, words or song refrains came to mind after your initial shock? Sing them now or write down a few of the words you remember.

4. Write a prayer or poem about "Hearing the News." Don't think, just write....

CHAPTER 2

NOW WHAT?

Lord God, I can hardly breathe
I can hardly believe
that You are with me.
Are You?
Lord God, I'm frozen
trapped in fear
that this is Your will.
Is it?

For weeks, I kept pressing the "Rewind Button" over and over in my head. Somehow thinking that if I replayed my conversation enough, HR would make my position, my paycheck, my benefits, and my colleagues magically reappear. I kept wondering what I could do and whom I could talk with to correct this "obvious" error. Was I really expendable? Was I only an expense on a profit statement? The honest answer was YES—even though I didn't want to admit it.

Do you feel like you're wearing concrete boots when you really need a life jacket? We can know that God is present in our lives, but there are times when well-intentioned words from family and friends aren't enough. I wondered where the Lord was leading me. "God never closes a door without opening another." It was painful to hear, even if it was true.

I found comfort as I remembered that I was not alone in my job loss. The simple act of waking up and getting out of bed became a powerful exercise of hope. It was a rehearsal of faith, despite the nearly 10% unemployment statistics that surrounded me. When I took time to breathe deeply and connect with the rest of humanity, I felt a genuine connection to my nearly 15,000,000 new "friends" who were sitting in homes around the country scouring job postings, and praying for open doors—just like me.

As the shock of losing my job wore off, I realized how deeply I had given in to the pressure to overwork at the expense of my health, the well-being of my family members, and long-term friendships. "Produce, succeed, and get to the top" was a message I had swallowed hook, line, and sinker. But no more!

Losing my job became a chance to say "No" to positions that didn't match my strengths, my skills, or my passion. Even though I wasn't sure what the financial ending would look like, I found myself becoming more and more open to possibilities as I realized that I was not merely a job description or a list of tasks. Neither are you.

Caring

It feels like a weight around me, O God
　　this letting go
　　　　if only I could stop caring

Then it would be easier
　　to say goodbye
　　　　and move on in my life

But I can't move on
　　not just yet
　　　　because of the love I feel

Real love for my team and colleagues
　　they're the best
　　　　and I care so much

Bless them, O God, with hearts
　　open and free
　　　　rooted in the past & looking forward

Limits

I'm so proud, Lord
    I started to say, "No"
    and the world didn't end
    and neither did I

Losing a job is not the end
    not a death sentence
    and certainly not
    passive waiting

I said "No"
    and found freedom
    inner peace
    and a world of possibility

By setting limits
    to this severance period
    I'm creating space
    for real life

Thank you, Lord
    for helping me
    to stop being
    a "Yes" man

Speak Up

Conformity sucks, O God
I've spent my entire life
fitting in, standing in line
trying not to stand out

I hid my passion
by deferring to others
playing the game
by their rules

And now I hear a voice
Your Voice within me
calling me, no, pushing me
to stand up and speak out

I know this is true
Your Word is true
And I become true
by saying the words

Out loud,
no hiding this time
no fear of fitting in
or stealing the show
It's Your show after all

And I'm simply inviting others
to join the chorus
to scream with delight
at Your love waiting for us

God's Will

Lord, I'm waiting
What's the next step of the Journey?
Which way shall I turn?

I've heard it said if you want
to know God's will,
"Your phone will ring!"

I'm ready and waiting, Lord
Call Forwarding is ON

Wouldn't it be wonderful if your termination notice came with an envelope from the Lord that announced your new position and included the salary increase you really deserve? But life and faith just don't work that way. Congratulations on hanging in there as the shock of unemployment gives way to the daily grind of self-doubt and the freedom to reinvent yourself. Use this time of reflection to listen to your truest, deepest self, and to the Holy Spirit tugging you toward self-discovery.

It is OK to question, wonder, and even lament during this time of loss. What do you need to learn right now that will set the stage for your future? Thanks for staying in the moment and committing to this hard inner work.

For Reflection

1. Make a list of past memories that weigh you down. Burn or shred the list.

2. Write down the priorities in your job hunt. What is essential? Say "NO" to the rest.

3. Reach out to a mentor, counselor, or pastor to help you discern the voice of the Spirit as you wade through the stigma of unemployment.

4. Who in your life needs to hear from YOU?

CHAPTER 3

THE NEW NORMAL

All I can think of is "What happened?"
I want my life, my job, my paycheck back, Lord
My daily routine is gone
Is this really Your plan for my life?

As the buzzer went off, my wife said, "Why did you set your alarm? You don't have to be anywhere today." I sat on the edge of the bed and realized—No—I DON'T have to be anywhere today…I don't have a JOB! Do you feel like you are in limbo? Is the weight of losing your job keeping you under the covers and hiding from emotions you don't want to face?

I've never worked for a company that offered employee training in "What to Do When We FIRE You." There are no guidelines, no rules, and now I had no clear direction for being unemployed. I think they call this "transition."

In the first days and weeks after losing my job, I often felt "stuck" in the emotions that rolled over me every hour. I would remind myself to breathe and often had to take several loooooong breaths to keep myself centered and focused. I was amazed how quickly I could spin from self-pity to hope for revenge, then frustration, followed by a good dose of rage, and finally bewilderment—All during my morning coffee.

Then, my phone would ring, or I would receive an email filled with words of support and encouragement. Even though I had felt abandoned in the Land of Unemployment, I realized I was not alone…What a relief! Thank you, Holy Spirit!

If you're used to being busy and working hard, it's a daily challenge to let feelings and thoughts wash over you, and maybe even experience tears of shock, grief, and gratitude. Not knowing what is coming next can be a frightening place. When you add the stress of figuring out unemployment benefits, Work Force Center training, or the stark reality that you have NO benefits, transition becomes more than an intellectual concept. It is a journey of faith and trust.

It was hard for me to think long-term while I was worrying about unpaid bills and whether I should cancel our morning newspaper to reduce unnecessary expenses. In reality, I was learning the important balance between being IN the moment and keeping myself sustained with perspective. I invite you to allow these prayers to serve as anchor points while you find your "sea legs" and figure out the next steps in your career. You won't find instant answers, but you may realize you are not alone. God is with you, even though your faith may be shaken. Listen to your family and friends when they say, "It will be all right." The truth is, it will.

The Tower of Babel

It's a long line, Lord
and it seems uphill all the way
The chorus of voices around me
speaks languages I do not know...

Is that Spanish or Portuguese?
French or some Cajun dialect?
What's that street slang and what
are they saying?

It's a long line, Lord
and I'm ready to present my case
Documents, identification, and proof
that I am unemployed

What? I need to come back?
AFTER my severance has ended?
But Lord, the line was long
and I waited. I really waited

So much for being proactive
in the Tower of Babel

I will learn to navigate this maze
It's amazing how one single, orderly line
can bring comfort and connection to those around me

Lord, remind me that I am a part
of everyone I meet, of their story
of their hopes, and hurts, and dreams

Teach me to wait, Lord
Because there's a long line ahead of me

What to Say

"I meant to call," he said,
"But I didn't know what to say."

Lord, it's like talking to someone
facing cancer, or another illness

That awkward feeling of wanting
to connect but not being able

To step inside the other's shoes
And truly feel what's going on

Don't let this job-ending,
this transition, keep people away

I want, I need to be connected
to simply be listened to

I don't need to be fixed
or have the problem solved

I just need someone who will
be a part of the Journey

And silent presence is
OK with me, Lord

What's the Score?

I know the Canticle says,

"The heavens are telling the glory of God,
and all creation is shouting for joy.
Come, dance in the forest, come, play in the field,
and sing, sing to the glory of the Lord."

But what if I'm not sure of my part right now?
Lord, what if I don't know the notes
for this point in life?
What if I get it all wrong?

I see You waving your arms
trying to conduct this grand musical
and keep us all on the same page
But I can't read the score,
the notes aren't clear right now

And what if I make a mistake...

Are You keeping score, like a cosmic test?
Will I measure up if I play my part
and it doesn't fit Your plan?

Lord, help me to trust Your Divine wisdom
and the vision You've planted deep in my heart

Let me join in the chorus of creation's song
bringing glory to Your holy Name!

The Blessing

Do You ever get tired of all the "asking" Lord?

Do Your ears burn from the myriad pleas born of
ego, desire, lust, and pure greed?
And those are just mine.

Are we missing the point
of Your intention to bless
ALL that You created?

Help us, Dear God, to receive what is best for us.
In that holy cycle of giving and receiving may
we find peace and true contentment.

Draw us near to You, O Lord.
That is the truest blessing.

And give us the presence of mind
and heart to shut up
And say, "Thank you!"

Head Bowed

Father, into Your hands I commend my spirit
and my talents and dreams

Take what I thought was "me"
And make it new

Into something...You can use
and something I can use

My head is bowed
and my heart is open

Your will be done
and quickly wouldn't hurt

Amen

D on't you wish you had a compass that would automatically give you directions for how to navigate through unemployment? The truth is that the path is different for everyone. More than once, I simply wanted to call it quits and give in to my fear, doubt, and misplaced anger. Just ask my wife and my cousins who housed us or my friends—they saw the truth of my frustration.

I eventually realized that I needed to embrace the ending of my job, then be willing to wait, and THEN be open to a new beginning. Wouldn't it be great to immediately go from losing your job to working for the best boss you could ever hope to find? Good luck with that. The rest of us will have to embrace our "closed door" and sort through the lessons there for us to learn. Here are some things to think about as you realize your job ending is real. The good news is that God's presence is also real. Remember that as you wait for a new door to open.

For Reflection

1. Go back to your notes or drawings from "Hearing the News." What do you notice? What feelings or thoughts come to mind? Write them down.

2. Step away from your job search and go for a walk. The simple act of putting one foot in the front of the other can remind you that your life has purpose—Even if that purpose isn't entirely clear right now. Get moving...

3. Who would you like to talk to right now? Call a friend who can listen to you for 10 minutes. Then use every second to say what is happening in your life.

4. Find a place where you can listen to your soul. What words or images come to mind? Stop pleading for God's help—just for a moment. Is there something you need to let go of inside? Write it down.

CHAPTER 4

WHERE'S MY MAP?

Lord Jesus Christ, Son of the Living God,
where in the world are you?

Show Yourself please
and have mercy on me, a sinner!

Do you like roller coasters? If you do, then losing a job and lurching into the unknown of waiting is for you! But if you get motion sickness from carnival rides, you might not fare as well. Does ANYONE really like being unemployed? It can be hard to relax, trust, and find your "own" daily routine when a job ends. I was grateful for the weekday ritual of looking for job leads on the Internet, doing research, calling references, taking time to walk, and preparing family meals. You might have been used to a different schedule with split shifts or project-based work. Find out what works for YOU now. Unemployment is not a one-size-fits-all experience.

I made a conscious choice to be patient and trust the new normal in my life. I also remembered to look around to find out where I could share my gifts and give something back to the community. Volunteering became therapeutic for me as I focused on someone else and realized that I had something worthwhile to share. As I listened to the needs of others, I stopped thinking as much about "poor me." So, get busy! Give what you can where you can to those who have less than you.

Your time of transition can be more than a hunt for income. You can make it a time to discern, learn from past mistakes, create new patterns of health, and discover deeper relationships. After several hours of concentrated job searching, to make sure I met the guidelines for my unemployment payment, I would reach out to long-lost friends, call colleagues to thank them for their collaboration, and spend time writing. A wise writer and friend once told me that the secret to writing was, "Keep your butt in the chair" and DO IT! My unemployment gave me the time and space to do just that.

My daily activities became a healthy routine and my new normal. By stepping back and connecting the dots, I noticed a new pattern in my life. I was creating a map to an unknown destination by the very act of daily living. The future we seek while we are unemployed is created one day at a time, one phone call, and one conversation at a time. That's how the Holy Spirit works! What path can you create during your time of transition?

Prayer for Balance

L: *Left brain*
R: *Right brain*

L: I think I know all of the answers and just what to say, Lord
Just let me ponder a little more and things will be clear

R: I feel lost and confused with all the possibilities before me, Lord
Help me to stop thinking so hard and simply trust You

L: Actually, I think if I just work a little harder
things will get better, Lord
Maybe a bit more order and organization in my life will help?

R: But then I sense Your hand guiding me in unseen
but real ways, Lord
A phone call or email from friends brings needed peace
and inner calm

L: But maybe I'm not networking enough; should I be
working harder, Lord?

Missing the Mark

Lord, I hate tests
The pressure to produce and the long preparation
causes so much stress

Lord, even more, I hate life-tests
That crashing headlong into the American dream
of Life, Liberty, and Lots of Stuff

But You know my heart like no other, Lord
and I have failed in Your sight
and in front of so many around me

The sin of my life is ever before me
MY will not Thine I have done
and in the end I've missed the mark

Wipe away the tears of sorrow, Lord
and hear my plea for healing and hope
Restore in Your servant a heart to serve You

Take this broken arch and bridge the gap
I have created between us
so I may stand ready for the next test

Amen

Life Jacket

It's been years since I've been in a canoe
On the water

I re-member Bob's paddle instructions…
The C-stroke, a pry, and "feathering" the paddle
All the while grateful for my PFD…
Personal flotation device.

Well Lord, I'm in open water now
And feeling quite alone
Sure Bob is with me "in spirit"
but it's just me, the water—and my PFD

Thank You, Lord for all of the times
You provided
the answer I needed

Showed the way
when I was lost

I'm learning not to be proud
I'll take any help You offer

Just show me the way to the next shore

Help Me to Learn

Lord, I've heard the wisdom:
"We teach best that which we most need to learn."

No wonder I'm such a good teacher
I have sooo much to learn

Still there are times
when I think I know it all

Or think I'm competent enough
To "fake" my way through

But now is the time to be real
No more guessing and halfhearted truths

Help me to be honest, Lord
and open enough to ask the hard questions

I will listen with all my heart, mind, and soul
if You will tell the Spirit to "speak up!"

My Angry Prayer

Lord, I'm really afraid
   the fear is deep inside
   and it comes out "sideways"
     as anger

I want to rage against this dark night
   this paralyzing fear
   but control isn't working
     so far

Help me surrender to Your will
   to truly accept each moment
   of every day and help me to
     let go

In Words

John's letter came on Valentine's Day
A rare, handwritten note expressing
fondness and affirmation
for our years of work
together

Thank you for John's wisdom, Lord
"I want to let you know 'in words'
How much I feel for you."

A welcome gift of empathy

Leaving a job and the security
of work's familiarity—
is a scary and lonely place
to be.

John's note brought gratitude

And now I find freedom, Lord
Beyond mere comfort, I am
energized to pursue new dreams
and act on the Spirit's tug toward
peace

Make my life a witness to You
May my actions bear the truth
of the words I speak
and affirm the power of making a
difference

Le Voyage

It's been a long journey
    are we there yet?
When will this traveler
    find a place to rest?
When will I be "at home"
    and at peace with myself?

It's been a long journey
    and I want to be settled
I'm impatient, Lord
    and find it hard to trust You

Help me be true to the Journey
    the path You've set before me

                Amen

During my early years in youth ministry, I was part of a talented group of "outdoor" friends. Denis, Duane, Jim, and I led groups of teens and young adults on wilderness backpacking adventures. On a trek in the Bighorn Mountains of Wyoming, we encountered a fellow hiker along the trail. He introduced himself as "Larry-Dirt-Eatin'-Johnson." He seemed to be a genuine "mountain man" and had us at hello.

It turned out that Mr. "Dirt-Eatin'" was actually an accountant from Denver who spent a month each summer in the wilderness and lived off the land. We invited him to join us for an evening of dehydrated cuisine. During dinner, one of the teens asked Mr. Johnson if he had ever been lost.

There was a pregnant pause, then Larry, who traveled with no maps and limited camping gear responded "I've never been LOST but I have been 'POWERFUL CONFUSED'—for a week or two!" Unemployment offers a similar challenge as we try and find our way. Remember you are not alone, even if you feel like you are lost.

Use these questions to help you discern the Holy Spirit's guidance in your life.

For Reflection

1. Recall a time when you were lost or "powerful confused." Who did you ask for direction? What was the outcome?

2. Where do you find comfort and hope even though your future may not yet be clear?

3. Is there a way you can serve others while you job hunt? Can you volunteer in your church, a community program, or local school?

4. What are you doing to maintain your relationships with colleagues or friends? Who do you miss—near or far? Is there someone with whom you can "check in" on a regular basis?

CHAPTER 5

LETTING GO

Waiting
feels eternal

Hoping
the end will come

Let go

My unemployment offered the gift of a cross-country move. Our home sold quickly, so we packed up everything we owned and drove several THOUSAND miles to stay with my cousin in Seattle. Driving was the best reality therapy my wife and I could have imagined. Each mile we drove became a stark reminder that a chapter in our lives was ending and new pages were about to be written. Because we weren't distracted by all of our "stuff," we found it easier to embrace the change unemployment had brought to our lives. We had dreamed of making this move for years, and now unemployment provided the kick we needed to do it. The hand of God brought us to a new address with a real chance to "let go" of the past. We had prayed for twenty years to be close to extended family. Our prayer was answered in a phone call that announced my termination. The ending of my job opened up a whole new world for my family and me.

We were fortunate to have our house sell right away. Your new life as a job seeker might include a mortgage payment and a gas gauge eerily close to EMPTY. On top of the pressure to keep your family intact, you may also be facing an internal tension to hold on to lost dreams, lost recognition, and the loss of freedom to buy things when you want to or need to. Life may not be turning out how you thought it was going to be. If you don't WANT to let go of that, it's OK. Transition takes time... Take all the time you need.

When I was stripped of the things I had held dear—financial security, career status, employee recognition, and support—I found my way back to the people who really mattered most in my life. I was given a great gift when I was forced to keep my ego in check while living on a weekly unemployment payment. It didn't feel like a gift at the time, but when the dust settled, I realized that I had ALL that I needed. My family, close friends, and the still-small presence of God.

Beyond the Headlights

It's possible to drive in the dark
    all night long
All it takes is good headlights...
    200 feet at a time

Lord, help me to see beyond
    my current situation
And not be limited by doubt
    or inner fear

Help me to trust You, O Lord
    and move forward
Knowing my destination
    is just ahead

Around the corner

Downsizing

Lord, thanks for the revelation
that we have too much stuff
In fact we have stuff in storage
just to make room for new stuff

I think I'm tired of being "stuffed"
and it's time to make room

Room for things that matter
like long-lost friends and
a niece needing a call at college

Room for walks around the lake
and taking the time to buy fresh food
that really feeds the soul

Lord, thanks for the insight
that a big house and pool
is a luxury at the expense
of stewardship and service

I can do more with less
and You can do more with me

Amen

Homeless

I didn't think the house would sell that quickly, Lord
I mean, two weeks—
    That was fast.

It was anticlimactic to do all of the prep,
make the place look pretty,
    And then it SOLD

So now the "letting go" begins, the packing
and sorting and realization
    We are homeless

The move is set, storage is arranged
and we will live with cousins
    Time for Chosen Family

Thank You for the freedom that has come
in getting rid of the STUFF accumulated over the years
    Making room for You!

Help us to listen hard during this pilgrimage
To give what we can in the spirit of gratitude

Amen

Thinking Outside the Box(es)

It's sinking in, Lord
We are soon to be homeless
    and that's a good thing.

I never dreamt I'd feel
this kind of freedom
    What a gift.

The boxes are stacked
They fill every room
    Stuff waiting to go.

After the "Moving Sale"
We will take
    very little with us.

How did we ever think
We could not
    live without all this STUFF?

And now that we are letting go
Thinking outside the boxes
    we see new possibilities.

Having less to move around
    is making room in our hearts
    for new dreams and visions.

Please connect the dots, Lord
and be close by
during this "moving" experience!

    Amen

As a young adult, I visited my local prison and played guitar at the Sunday services. Little did I know a member of my own family would later be incarcerated. I learned a lot about family systems during that time and saw the power of faith, personal change, and conversion firsthand. Unemployment gave me the time to reconnect with my previous experience at the prison and give something back again. Every Monday evening I began to surrender my own freedom and visit the state prison as a volunteer with the Concerned Lifers Organization (CLO). The CLO is a group of men who have sentences over twenty-five years. Many of them are living "life without parole." As I began listening to their stories of absent fathers, limited education, mental illness, alcohol and drug abuse, and the impact of horrendous crimes on victims and families, I realized how much these men wanted to belong in society. I heard a loud communal cry from them. These men would give anything to give back something for their crimes.

When I was privileged to hear these stories, I felt a deep connection to God's creation. I realized that these men were also children of God, even if society wanted to throw away the key and punish them instead of finding a way to repair the harm they had afflicted. As I visited with these men and let go of my freedom each week, I walked out of the prison and past the razor wire with a profound sense of renewal. I received much more than I gave each week. It was another reminder to me that God was working.

For Reflection

1. How can your skills and strengths help you do something new with your life or career?

2. What are the biggest distractions draining your energy these days? Write them down.

3. Who or what do you rely on when you can't see your way in life? What role does your faith play in your life?

4. Have a rummage sale and get rid of the extra STUFF in your life. Donate what doesn't sell to an organization in need.

PART II

SURPRISED BY RENEWAL

CHAPTER 6

BEYOND DISTRACTION

*O God, I'm stuck in the middle
of this struggle to find the way,
Your Way.*

*Renew Your Spirit within me
that I may find Your path
and follow.*

Amen.

As the weeks turned into months and the months seemed like an eternity, I realized that my unemployment was part of the national news. Each night, a friendly face behind the news desk would report on jobs lost and modest gains in certain job market segments. The statistics became a sort of "code" for me. As I heard 10% unemployment lowering to 9.5% and then 9%, I became 100% certain that I was connected with every job seeker in the United States.

I experienced a newfound clarity that I was not alone in the land of unemployment. Neither are you. Something strange actually began happening inside of me and in my family. During the early months of my unemployment adventure, I found it hard to concentrate. I knew it was a symptom of grieving, and I tried to cut myself some slack. But still it happened.

My momentary lapses of concentration usually took the form of staring out the window into our wooded yard. It was easy to get lost in a flood of "What if...," "I should have...," and "Lord please..." Then the phone would ring and bring me back to the tasks and emotions at hand. Are you finding it hard to focus? Do you fall into spells of daydreaming? Welcome to the challenge of "waiting." This is the time between losing your job and finding a new place to use your gifts and talents.

The clarity that I was not alone did not give instant reassurance, but I felt a quiet trust. I thought about the time Jesus spent in the desert and the temptations he faced to be relevant, spectacular, and powerful. In the Scriptures, the wilderness, *eremos* in Greek, was a place to confront "demons" and the inner "beasts" of ego and pride that keep us from saying "yes" to God's healing grace.

By paying careful attention to the lessons I was learning each day, a new focus began to emerge that was accompanied by hope, confidence, and an abiding trust. The grief and sadness of losing my job was giving way to something new. The "new" wasn't clear, but in my heart of hearts something told me that I would be OK. I came to realize that it was the work of the Holy Spirit tugging me toward wholeness.

Open the Door

I know You stand at the door and knock
 so why do I hesitate to open?

Why don't I recognize Your presence
 in the world, in my midst, in my heart?

I understand the dynamic, in my head
 that strangers become guests
 and guests become friends
 who become brothers & sisters

But I don't open the door
 and miss the grace
 of Your love that has the power
 to make a stranger a friend

Lord, teach me to love, really love
 and open the door

Of my heart held shut, mind locked
 Afraid of the waiting gift

A Channel of Your Peace

We frighten easily these days, O God
>   we run
>   we hide
>   we curse the day of our Baptism
>   and long to evade Your creative call

We fill our lives with meaningless things, O Lord
>   we shop
>   we buy
>   we consume to hide the fear
>   of surrender to Your all-consuming love

But if we pause and stop the noise
>   we listen
>   we rest
>   we find peace in connecting
>   to Your ever-present love & grace

Give me, O God, the heart of Saints Francis & Clare
>   to surrender
>   to receive
>   to act on the unlimited potential that comes
>   in being a channel of Your peace

Whisper in My Ear

I can't take it anymore, Lord
This constant NOISE
    is driving me crazy

Stop laughing, I KNOW
I'm ALREADY crazy
    but I need Your help

Save me from the addiction
to fill my life
    with sound & the louder the better

Free me from this compulsion
To fill every minute
    with busy distraction

I want peace and I want it
NOW, deep in my soul
    soothing all the rough spots

Aaaaaaah, there You are
The comfort of Your Whisper
    as soft as my breath

Another deeeep exhale
and I feel at rest
    please whisper in my ear

Be Still

I know all the right stuff
   in my head, Lord

Getting it into my heart,
   well that's another matter

Losing my job, my busy work
   has given me pause

Literally, time to be still
   and know that I'm NOT God

Stop laughing, Lord
   this is a tough lesson

And one that I've resisted
   by staying busy

But now I'm quiet
   and my heart is still

And here it is
   the mystery revealed

Listening is allowing me to hear
   and thus obey Your call

I know all the right stuff
   In my heart, Lord

Eye to Eye

Now that the distractions are gone
I am free to really notice the people and things
around me

I'm sorry, Lord
I've been so busy with all of the URGENT
stuff in my life and with work
that I forgot the IMPORTANT things

My daily walks have become a place of reflection
A look in the mirror of my soul and a chance to gaze
at the world You have created

Thank you for meeting me "Eye to eye and heart to heart"
The still small voice of your Spirit is as close to me as my
very life-breath. I am filled with gratitude

Looking up from the walking path
I finally take the time to notice (reverence)
the beauty of Your creation

Grandparents tending children at the slide,
parents pushing strollers,
and my walking-path comrades trying to shed
the heaviness of work and loss carried across the years

Face to face I glance
and learn to gaze, to ponder, to wonder,
and be filled with amazement at the
beauty of life that surrounds me

Thank You for greeting me in the faces of those around me
I'm so glad that we are finally seeing "eye to eye."

Walking saved my life. On the days that Margo went to work, I took over a small bedroom in my cousins' home that doubled as a home office. Mornings were my time to search for jobs, complete applications, and reach out to friends and networks of contacts. The afternoon was my time to walk.

Gene Coulon Memorial Beach Park sits serenely on the southeast shore of Lake Washington, about twenty-five minutes from Seattle. Like most public parks, Gene Coulon Park offers picnic and playground areas. Unlike most parks, the setting for the walking trails includes scenic views of Mount Rainier, the Olympic Mountains, and Lake Washington boat ramps. The park also includes one special resident, Sam.

As my walking became a regular routine, I noticed a bearded man who walked the park and carried plastic bags. We would pass each other each day, and eventually I began to say, "Hi." He would never respond in kind, so one day I asked a local vendor about my trail companion. I found out his name was Sam. Sam was homeless and lived within the confines of the park. His father had drowned in the lake when he was a child and he remains locked in the effects of the trauma. After some time, I was able to confirm Sam's schedule and provide him with a winter coat, new tennis shoes, bags of food, and other clothing.

Sam still walks Gene Coulon Park and survives with the support of neighbors. Seeing him reminds me to focus on what really matters in my life and to make a small difference whenever I can. *Lord, thank you for Sam. Keep him safe and bring healing to his life.*

For Reflection

1. What am I afraid of in my life? How does fear keep me from exploring new career options?

2. Who needs to hear the words, "I'm sorry" and "I love you" from you? Reach out to them...

3. If God were to write a love letter to you, what would it say? What do you want to hear most?

4. Give yourself the gift of one morning away from the phone, computer, and TV. Calm your mind and listen to the tug of the Holy Spirit. Write down the words and images that come to mind.

CHAPTER 7

CREATED TO BE

You, O Lord, are the God who leads me
You, O Lord, are the God who frees me
You, O Lord, are the God of my being

How's your job search going? Are you spending any time at your local Work Force or Unemployment Resource Center? Isn't it amazing to sit in the waiting room and watch the banks of computers churning out every possible job connection?

I waited for an hour in our local unemployment support office and then sat in the cubicle of my "career counselor." She looked at my educational background and stared at her computer. Then, she scoured my work history and experience and let out a loooong sigh...Finally, she looked at my salary history, paused, and then turned her head toward me. As our eyes met, she said two words, "Good luck."

She went on to say that I was overqualified and should expect to take at least a 50% salary cut in the current economy. How's that for a confidence builder? I did appreciate her honesty however. After that reality check, my career guide took time to make a genuine personal connection as she said the most important words of all, "Tell me about your strengths."

What are your "real" strengths? When are you MOST energized? Do you find yourself thinking, "I could do that?" as you look at job postings and pore over the Want Ads? Have you spent hours making changes to your cover letter and résumé to match the "keywords" in a job description so that your résumé will be noticed?

You may be tempted to take a job that's not the best "fit" while looking for any opportunity to pay your bills or support your family. But is it worth enduring long hours, staff tensions, and daily unfulfilled repetition? When we remember God's original plan for our job hunting, it is much more than finding a paycheck. I know, that's easier said than done.

While you're knee-deep in résumé changes and figuring out what you want to DO with your life, I invite you to reflect on who you want to BE. Follow your strengths. Doors will open...

Never Mind

What were you THINKING, O God?
What was on Your mind when You spoke the words,
　　"Let there be…?"

How much Sabbath-inspired rest did it take
To muster those creative, saving thoughts?
　　"Let there be…?"

You, the Divine *Logos* who became
The Word made flesh. Did You mean it when You said,
　　"Let there be…?"

I hope You don't mind all the questions,
And my doubting-Thomas fears of hearing
　　"Let there be…"

Because it's hard to quiet my mind and heart and soul
and hear the real intention of Your creative voice,
　　"Let there be…"

Overflowing Life

It's easy to get frozen, Lord
    paralyzed and stuck
Heavy with the guilt of the past
    avoiding fear of the future

And so I hide from You, O Lord
    hoping You won't notice
Praying others keep You busy
    with "divine distraction"

But who am I kidding?
    Certainly not You, Lord
You know the pulse of my heart
    and every hair I'm losing

You shatter my dumbstruck fear
    with the healing reminder
I AM Your created one
    Your life overflows in me

Thank You for the gift
    of this eternal NOW
And the love that spills over
    the dam of my heart

Your Power in Me

The Quantum physicist and the theologian
   use the same words
   to describe You, O God...

You are the Energy that can never
   be created or destroyed

You are Everything that ever existed
   and will ever exist

You are always moving in form,
   through form, and out of form

You are the Infinite Field of Possibility

But right now, at this moment
   I'm tired, Lord

I need Your Power, Your Eternal
   Energy to keep me going

Right now, at this moment
   I'm focused on ME, O God

And I need Your Eternal perspective
   to see the big picture

To trust that this is not the end
   but a chance to know
   Your power in me

STicK PeOpLe

We live in a world that doesn't like dreamers, Lord
 and so we forget the Vision
 planted deep within
 every cell of our being

Being creative brings criticism
and explanations
 so we play it safe
 not using our voices
 to color Your world

Take away the fear inside, Lord
 and help us claim
 the confidence that comes
 in being Children of God

Thank You for re-minding us
 we don't have to be the BEST artist
 all we have to do is
 come out and play

Both/And

I grew up with an artist's heart, Lord
    the seed You planted
    expressed itself in music

Learning the notes and clefs
    the key signatures
    and playing together

Opened a new world to me
    and unlocked the code
    of Your Divine language

Yet in my head I've battled
    with my imagination
    thinking knowledge more important

Trying to be logical
    and practical in life
    not being TOO creative

But now there's so much inside
    waiting to come out
    longing for expression

Help me to judge less, Lord
    and simply open
    my heart to Your gifts

May they honor You
    and bring the inspiration
    to play well with others

Michelangelo's sculpture of "David" is a Renaissance masterpiece that stands seventeen feet tall in Florence, Italy. Its impact however, lies not in its ultimate beauty and proportion, but because David is presented without the defeated head of Goliath. He stands as "David"— alone.

World travelers flock to Florence to see Michelangelo's art, but Margo and I decided to journey to Vinci, in Tuscany. There we found a small museum built around Michelangelo's childhood home. It showed his masterful blending of science and art, but what struck me most was the story told about the statue of David.

An admirer watched as Michelangelo chiseled into a massive piece of Italian marble. Upon completion of the work, Michelangelo was asked, "How did you KNOW David was in there?" Michelangelo replied, "I simply chipped away all that was NOT David!"

God is doing the same with each of us—particularly during this time of job seeking. Little by little we find God's "David" inside of us as we return to our real selves beyond the distractions of work. With each job application, we can reflect on our gifts and talents, hopes and dreams. Unemployment is difficult and filled with stress, yet it can be full of grace.

For Reflection

1. Do you have a hobby or artistic gift that you have neglected while working or amid the urgency of job hunting? How can you express that gift?

2. What's your favorite hymn or psalm? Find the lyrics in a book or on the Internet and use them as a prayer this week.

3. You've spent lots of time updating your résumé. Now take some time to write your obituary. How would you like to be remembered? Describe your values, commitments, and life goals. How does your job seeking match the way you want to live your life?

4. Finish this sentence: I feel strongest and safest when...

CHAPTER 8

PERSPECTIVE

Lord, give me eyes to see the Truth
ears to hear Your Word
a mouth to proclaim Your Goodness
And hands to make a difference
in Your world.

Have you ever had one of those days when you felt "behind"—all day long—and no matter how you hurried, organized, or prioritized, it all just seemed to fall apart? I had a day like that. It started with an early-morning flight from Dallas to Los Angeles.

I hadn't anticipated the morning weather would bring traffic to a crawl. I nearly missed my flight and gratefully settled into seat 5C with thoughts of a lengthy nap in flight. As I clicked my seat belt, I heard a gentle rain falling on the polished aluminum of the airplane. Off I dozed…

Three hours later, I heard a loud DING and jumped out of my seat to grab my luggage and deplane. The only problem was that we were still in DALLAS! A morning thunderstorm had closed the runways and I slept through the whole thing. "O Lord, please…" was my first lament!

When we finally landed in Los Angeles, I literally ran to the car rental shuttle with hopes that my "Executive, super-dooper, carbon-fiber-teflon-coated, double-platinum" status would help me avoid the Rental Counter and get to the presentation I was about to MISS.

Heart racing and short of breath, I settled my car into the LA traffic, restraining myself so that I wouldn't drive TOO fast. And there he was. A car in front of me driving MUCH slower than the speed limit and swerving within his lane. I went from "zero to rage" in a few seconds and uttered a friendly expletive of encouragement. At that very moment, the contact in my left eye dropped onto my lap. "Great! PERFECT!"

So now I'm the one all the cars are passing and angrily gesturing at in frustration! When I finally got my contact back in place on my eye, I began to chuckle, and then LAUGH. Out LOUD! It wasn't an audible voice, but I could hear the still-small voice of the Holy Spirit and the Gospel of Matthew whispering in my ear, "Take the LOG out of your own eye before you take the SPECK out of your brother's."

I was so out of balance—so self-absorbed and so arrogant that my perspective was completely closed off to the world around me.

Unemployment can be a bit like me driving on the LA freeway—IF you let it! Sometimes it helps to step away from all of the tasks and requirements connected with your job search. Step away from your desk, your Internet connection, and your text messages—Just for a moment. Then take a long look into the distance and try to see the "big picture."

Taking a step back can help you see who you are and where you've recently been. Connect the dots of your family ties, the support of friends, and your trust in God's providence. Then be still and know that you're NOT God! It's always good to see the "big picture."

Silver Lining

You must have really enjoyed this one, Lord

The call from Sean came unexpected
A son calling his father
with words of comfort and encouragement

"You'll be OK, Dad!"
Those words felt like winning the lottery
(which I wouldn't mind experiencing, Lord)
and came as palpable love across the airwaves

What father doesn't pray for his children
every day, and often many times a day?
And what father doesn't dream about
seeing those children grow into free
and responsible adults?

If I hadn't lost my job
I'd never have received that call
That glorious, hope-filled, healing call
I'd have missed it

So thank you, Lord
for this silver lining
this unearned grace

And when do You think Sean
will be able to pay for his own phone?

Do Over

"You are so lucky," she said
"You get a 'Do over!'"

I hung up the phone, Lord
and let the truth sink in

This ending in my life
is just a new beginning

Like so many times
when You opened Your arms

And welcomed me back
with healing and forgiveness

This transition is a "Do over"
My chance to be honest and true

To the passion and dreams
I've hidden deep within

Thank you, Lord for revealing to me
The difference between a career and true vocation

Open my heart to listen and discern
Then let me follow Your lead

With courage, hope
and all the passion I can muster

Now I understand
that luck is not the same as being blest!

Solitude

It's just me, Lord
but I'm not alone

Thanks for Your ever-present
love that permeates everything

Everyone is working
and I'm alone

With You, the Alone
who lives in Community

Father, Son, and Spirit, guide me.

Above the Clouds

I've lived much of my life "above the clouds," Lord
    Workshops, meetings, training
    All starting and ending at the airport

I've taken for granted the quiet retreat
    that each flight brings "above the clouds"
    Millions of air miles to pause and just BE

Now that I'm unemployed and grounded for a while
    I can truly appreciate the gift You gave me
    by standing in lines and learning to wait

"Above the clouds" there are no lines on the maps
    only milky vapor separating earth and sky
    and my body, mind, and spirit merge

Seeing the "big picture" literally, is freeing
    and frightening at the same time
    No hiding from the truth "above the clouds"

Lord help me bring that truest, deepest part of myself
    back to earth, to my family and friends
    I want to live that connected life here & now

Going Deep

I look at the trees around me
    with utter amazement

They reach so high and stand as guardians
    over the wounded earth

These glorious sentinels stand tall
    yet reach deep into the ground

Down, down, down they go
    roots finding nourishment

And those very same roots reach out
    and connect to nearby trees

Forming a system, giving support
    becoming a community

Right now I don't feel rooted, Lord
    In fact I'm easily blown over

By stress and distraction
    and fear of the future

I want to go deep, much deeper
    but I'm afraid of what's there

Can You handle the truth
    of my darkest self?

Well now is the time, a Spirit-guided tug
    to let go and dig deep

Thank You, Lord for the rootedness of others
    who help me to stand tall

A Turn in the Road

Family taught me to work and play hard
    Caring for everyone and the earth
    responsible for pulling my own weight

Ministry taught me to listen and discern
    Building relationships with others & myself
    Welcoming God's gracious gifts

Business taught me to be productive and efficient
    Taking the shortest path, producing
      the most revenue
    Incurring the lowest cost

Unemployment is teaching me to be still and reflect
    Assessing the real quality of my life
    Getting rid of all the junk

Lord, I'd prefer a simple path
    Following a straight line and
    knowing all of the steps

But now there's another turn in the road
    Inviting me toward passion or comfort
    Daring me to choose

My recent job loss was not my first. Early in my career, a project came to an end, and funding did not continue, so I was out of work.

At the time, I didn't have the presence of mind to capture my thoughts in writing. But after the initial shock and panic, I decided to do some real discernment. Not long after, my phone rang. William was on the line offering me a position with an amazing team. Again, the Spirit came through and my family and I were off to a new chapter in a new setting. Another lesson for Doubting Timothy!

Maybe that's why I didn't panic when my recent job disappeared. My last experience gave me peace of mind even though I didn't know the final outcome.

Have you received a phone call that has you thinking, "Maybe I should….?" Have you met a new professional contact who's spurred energy you haven't felt for a while? Perspective isn't a mystical, magical gift. Just keep your eyes, ears, and heart open. The Spirit is working. You'll see.

For Reflection

1. Take a moment to name the "silver lining" blessings you experienced today, this week, this month…

2. What needs to be done around your house? Take some time for these chores. Pray for your unemployed sisters and brothers around the country as you work.

3. Finish this sentence: Lord, help me to see…

4. What would you do with your life if you had unlimited courage and resources?

CHAPTER 9

ACTIVE FAITH

Dream...Speak...Believe
Forgive...Welcome
Teach...Send...Comfort
Empty...Redeem

God, You are a Verb
the Action
behind every action

Acute Lymphocytic Leukemia — ALL. Sounds serious. It turns out it is. My best friend, Denis, and his wife, Pat, were with us visiting their new grandson and celebrating life. We thought Pat was weary from jet lag. Now we wish that had been the case.

The "Big C" has been a significant part of my life. Cancer took my brother, Father Michael, at the age of thirty-three. My parents, grandparents, uncles, and an aunt have all fought cancer as well. Margo and my son, Sean, have treatable skin cancer. And now Pat is fighting for her life.

During my fifteen months of job hunting, faith became a supportive gift and a challenge that wouldn't let me sit around and do nothing. Now Pat and Denis were beginning a similar journey. Their faith is keeping them strong, friends are reminding them that they are not alone, and they have a sense of quiet confidence that God IS in control.

Like a traumatic illness, unemployment is a major wake-up call! There's no room for sleeping in or "Buzz me tomorrow" when God calls, especially if it means a career shift or job that doesn't meet ALL of your expectations.

It takes faith to say "Yes" and then get busy and do the best you can, where you can, with what you have. I thank God that we don't have to believe alone. I always knew that faith was a personal decision. But it's never private. We are all in this together.

If it takes a village to raise a child and to support a cancer patient, the same holds true for unemployment. We all need a community of love to spur our belief into action while we are trying to find our way. As you reflect on your beliefs and the faith tradition that sustains you, consider what this time of job seeking is teaching you. Have you REALLY been abandoned, are you REALLY alone, will the right opportunity REALLY come along? It takes faith to walk in the dark and believe.

Too Silent Too Long

I've sensed Your Word deep in my heart
   since I was a child
      on the tip my tongue
         waiting for release

There was a time when it came out
   loud and clear
      played in orchestras
         sung in concerts

And then I went silent
   hidden in work
      healing the hurts
         spoken in anger

Thank You for giving me
   a new song
      to break the silence
         let's speak up!

Lord, let's make new music
   a song of co-creation
      bringing new life
         to the world.

Heavenly Hosts

Ever since I was a child, Lord
I knew that I was not alone

Someone, somewhere, somehow
was with me each step of the Way

Guiding me, tugging me
protecting me from harm

Sure, there were bumps and bruises
but I was never ever really hurt

So now I pause to thank You, O God
for my Guardian Angels, my Beings of Light

Across space and time
not limited by sight, touch, taste, hearing, or smell

Open my body, mind, & spirit
to their extraordinary protection and guidance

Teach me to welcome their revelation
Your Truth! here & now

May I learn to see clearly & hear the harmony
taste the goodness & smell the divine fragrance

That draws me home to You, O Lord
Thank You for my Heavenly Hosts!

"Eye has not seen, and ear has not heard,
...what God has prepared for those who love him."—1 Corinthians 2:9

Amen

The Driver's Prayer

There are those, O Lord, who call You the "Wind up" God
    setting the Universe in motion
    then stepping back to watch the show

Others take the incarnational view and call You
    Emmanuel, "God with us"
    or even better, "In it with us!"

As we continue to work out Your plan for creation
    I pause with gratitude
    for the gift and challenge of "Free will"

Thank You for the ability to mine the gifts and talents
    You've lavished upon me
    and then polish them in service to others

I re-member the story of the father
    who drove his family on a long
    vacation with the words…

"Let's stop to thank God for a safe trip"

Thank You for Your wise response —
    "Why thank Me? **You drove**!"

Let me never apologize for the gifts
    You've given to me and the dreams
    You planted in my heart

As I get busy with the tasks of Your call
    may I always be mindful of Your Spirit
    tugging me and then getting out of the Way

In the Vineyard

God of creation, You know the truth
    I love wine and the place it grows
    Such power in the grape's symbolic struggle...

Digging deep, pushing through hard soil
    searching for water and nourishment
    seeking stability for the growth
    that comes with bud break

Lord, it amazes me to watch
    the making of good wine,
    to see such committed discipline

Following the seasons and nature's cycle
    the vines are tended
    and exposed to nature's best
    as well as its predators

Allowing small clusters to grow
    with only natural support
    forces the best to survive
    and thrive with concentrated fruit

Thank You, God for the growth in my life
    for those who've pushed me deeper
    toward my truest, authentic self
    only to find You already there

Patiently and with great care, You cultivate
    the vineyard of my life
    my family, and friends, bringing
    new life to each season

Blessed be the God of the Vineyard!

The Promissory Note

I am in debt to You, O Lord
I owe You big time for…

A family that put the FUN
back into dysfunctional

A father who radiated joy
And loved his friends and work

A mother who worked through
her childhood by serving others

A brother who showed me
the real meaning of a change of heart

A priest-brother who taught me
That we "go to God" together

And a sister who understands
hospitality like no other

I am in debt to You, O Lord
for these roots and wings
All paid for with Your Word
made flesh now with us in Spirit

I am grateful God
for your promised covenant
That is never broken
even in my brokenness and sin

I will love You and serve You
all the days of my life.

I promise

Growing up on the Great Plains of the Dakotas was a great gift. The Mandan Indians lived just south of my hometown along the Missouri River. Lewis and Clark spent the winter with them on their journey west. Custer and the Seventh Cavalry encountered these native people before heading to the Little Bighorn, where their lives ended in battle.

The Lakota Indians of the Sioux tribes lived a bit farther south on the Dakota plains. In preparation for battle, Sioux warriors would dance and sing, "Hoka hey, hoka hey, hoka hey...." It meant "Today is a good day to die!" What a challenging way to live.

And it IS true. Any day is a good day to die when we believe we are loved. And according to God—we are! Any day is a good day to look for a job and find the best match for your abilities. Any day is a good day to wake up and use your gifts, talents, and strengths to make a difference—even if it is one small act.

For Reflection

1. Who or what has kept you going when you've been in despair or wanted to quit?

2. How were the seeds of faith planted in your life? What fruit do you see?

3. Read Matthew 4:4 on Monday, Romans 10:17 on Tuesday, Galatians 5:22–23 on Wednesday, Ephesians 5:15–17 on Thursday, and James 1:2–4 on Friday. Use these verses as a daily mantra.

4. Who in your life needs encouragement in his or her faith? Reach out…

CHAPTER 10

NEW LIFE

The sudden gift
of streaming tears,
A chance acquainting
with friends of old,
Listening and waiting
for the earth to say,
"Surprise!"

Each of us has what I call a "Board of Directors." Our lives are shaped by family, friends, teachers, church and community leaders, historical figures, saints, and sinners. We may not know all of them personally, but somehow they inspire us to choose the good, life-giving, and holy throughout our lives. They help us see the big picture and re-mind us to be true to ourselves and to our God.

Father Michael was the "Chairman of the Board" in my life for many years. He was one of those priests who understood hospitality and had a gift for helping people feel at home in his life and in the Church. Michael prayed and played hard. His world was not "either-or" but "both-and." He believed in the goodness of people and offered gracious forgiveness when it reared its ugly head. Michael was my brother. Literally.

When Michael was in the seminary, I entered the Catholic college across the street. I spent time with the seminarians and enjoyed their enthusiasm for the Church. The food at the seminary was also MUCH better than at my campus dining hall. Once a week, Michael would also take me out for dinner as a break from my studies. At the end of each meal, I'd reach for the check only to have Michael beat me to the punch. It became a game each week, as I would try to grab the bill before he could reach for it. Finally, the moment came when we both tugged at the ticket and held it in tension between us. Urging me to relent, Michael finally said, "Just shut up and say, 'Thank you!'"

That's the challenge of unemployment. I found it hard to be grateful when job hunting consumed the majority of my time. I often focused on what was missing from my life, rather than the goodness of who and what was right in front of me.

Are there days in your life when all you can think of is yourself and your fears as you stare out of the window, rather than trusting that God is active in your life? I had many days like that. Do your best to notice how God's grace comes into your life through people and support. Then shut up and say, "Thank you!"

You're Kidding Me

I re-member sitting at Jean Houston's feet, Lord
This woman-rabbi with a heart
    as large as Lake Superior
    and I re-member her laugh

There was overflowing joy
in the heart of this "both/and" woman
    this modern mystic
    who wasn't afraid to make connections

But even as she pushed the limits
of modern thinking
    She took the time
    to laugh and see that
    the joke's on us

We've met the enemy Lord,
And they ARE us, doubting
    Your always Present
    all Powerful & Knowing Love

You are the God of Jacob, and Timothy and Margo,
The God who Laughs
    to see beyond the impossible
    You gotta be kidding me!

Heartbeats

"We don't know if it's
a boy or girl, but we'll hear
the heartbeat next week!"

What an amazing phone call, Lord
to hear good news when my focus
has been blurred lately

O God, I pause right now
to center myself
and listen...

And there it is
my own heart beating
steady and strong

A reminder of Your presence
and our connection
at the very core of my being

Bless the young hearts
waiting to be born
a future unfolding

And welcome the old hearts
waiting to come Home
to rest in You

An Anniversary Prayer for Margo

Lord, so much changes over time
   yet so much stays the same

Over 30 years ago we spoke these words…

"Lord, we come this day to Your altar
A witness of Your Love
we share with all the world

Refrain: We give ourselves to each other & You
       Let there be one where there was two
       Let there be one

Lord, I thank You
For making this partner for me
With her I am whole, and in You we are One

Refrain: We give ourselves to each other & You
       Let there be one where there was two
       Let there be one"

A Prayer of Abundance—Psalm 8

O God,
   Your splendor and majesty overflow!

Everywhere I look
   I see Your beauty reflected
   Every sound seems to speak Your name
      even a small child's cry
      and children playing
      give voice to You!

At night when I look to the sky
   I am filled with wonder
   that You who created the Universe
      care for me
      You know me
      and I'm amazed

Deep inside I feel the Tug
   of Your Holy Spirit
   re-minding me again and again
      that I am created
      in Your image and likeness
      called to continue Your creative work

O God,
   Your splendor and majesty overflow!

Mille Grazie

Lord, do You ever grow weary of hearing us say, "Thank you?"

Whenever I pause, I'm struck with the realization

That everything I am and all that I have comes from You

Grazie!

Every breath I take and every glance at beauty is Your gift

And my responsibility is to savor and protect Your work

For all that You've given me and for all that is yet to come

Grazie!

As a college student I studied music performance. The deal was simple. Play the trumpet and get free tuition. Who wouldn't love that? My parents sure did.

Midway through my freshman year, I sensed a tug toward social work and ministry in the Church. From spending time with my brother, Michael, around the seminary, I knew that ordination was not my calling. Youth ministry became the direction I headed in.

A few years later, Michael was ordained. I'll never forget the reception that followed and the joy of witnessing Michael's life commitment. During the receiving line, a guest asked my father what it was like to have a priest in the family. My dad's next words continue to be such a gift to me. He replied, "I have TWO, only one's ordained." It was the ultimate affirmation for any son. My dad understood my call to serve the Church as a layperson, and his public affirmation expressed his faith in my career path. It was a powerful blessing.

We live in a world that rewards conformity. As children, we were reminded to stay inside the lines and not question. Only later in life are we sometimes invited to explore, imagine, and create. The God who made you, loves you, redeems you, and wants you to follow your strengths, your gifts, your instincts, and do what you love. That is how we can be a true human BE-ing!

For Reflection

1. Make a list of the "Board of Directors" in your life. Reach out with a phone call, card, or email to thank them for their influence and witness.

2. What have you become most grateful for during your time of un-employment? What didn't you expect?

3. Ask your family to talk about how your unemployment affects them. Be open—This isn't only about YOU. How can you support each other?

4. Write a psalm of THANKS. Pray it every day this week.

CHAPTER 11

A NEW HORIZON

The daffodils stand
in silent salute
Preparing the way
for summer's delight

Thank You, God
for helping me
to notice spring:
dark becomes light

As I write this final chapter, a friend and colleague of mine is dying. Bob has fought a courageous fight against leukemia and was fortunate enough to choose when the time was right for him to stop the treatments that have been keeping him alive. Outside my home, there are signs of spring and the sun's light lingers longer each day. Inside I am sharing a long-distance vigil with Bob's friends across the country. "Hoka hey" is no longer a historical phrase from my roots on the prairies. Now it is my farewell prayer for Bob as he goes to the "Big Healing" that awaits him with the angels and saints.

As I thought about Bob's dying, I took some time to reflect and listen. *Really* listen. My journey through unemployment was not a heroic accomplishment. I did not have any mystical visions or hear prophetic words. There was only the hard task of living one day at a time as I looked for work and gained a new appreciation for the support of my family, friends, and God's grace.

Unlike my friend, Bob, who chose when to stop his treatments, you didn't choose the time you would lose your job. It wasn't your decision to have your life thrown into a tailspin. You probably didn't pray, "Please God, teach me to trust You by taking away my livelihood, sense of self-esteem, and the ability to pay my bills."

I'm now employed and my life has turned a corner, but you may not have reached the same point in your journey—yet. You might be painfully stuck in the dark of an emotional "winter" with no spring or summer in sight. If so, do a reality check with me. Look around you...

Are you homeless? Have you been abandoned without support of ANY kind? Do you have food for today? Is there a place of worship near you? Do you have friends who will stand by you no matter what? Is there some kind of work you could do, even at a 75% pay cut? I'll bet there is. There was for me.

As we come to the end of our time together, I want to say, "Thank you" for opening your life, your heart, and your faith to this time of reflection and personal sharing. Take advantage of the self-awareness you've gained. Choose hope over fear and faith over despair. It's true that your view of life depends on where you sit. So get up, go outside, and walk beyond your present situation. God is waiting to see what you'll do with the gifts you've been given. Look with the eyes of faith and follow the Light that leads you. Follow the Light...

The Big Healing

Eat right. Exercise.
   Die anyway!

There's no way around it is there, Lord?
This "Big, Fat, Greedy" life of mine
   will come to an end.

Or is it really the End?

When I see my boys, now young men,
   and watch my nieces grow
I know that the Circle of Life is never-ending

In fact the joke's on us!

We run around, stay busy, and carry
   the dis-ease of our past with us
Failing to let go and travel light

Remind us, O God, that you hold Eternity
   in the palm of Your hand
Our dying is really the Big Healing!

Treadmill

I am amazed, O God, at the calm I feel
    in the midst of unemployment
I mean really calm, an inner peace
    I've not felt in years

What a strange gift this transition has been
    time to pause and reflect
Like a long overdue sabbatical
    there's finally room in my soul for You

I'm off the treadmill of activity and urgency
    and filled with real rest
A constant state of "Sabbath" with the freedom
    to simply BE

Thank You, O God, for this mindful pause
    and time to focus
    on the important people and things
    in my life

I knew I was stressed out
    but couldn't "name it"
Until the treadmill stopped and I was
forced to step off

Mea Culpa

I'm sorry that I haven't trusted You, Lord
I've resisted Your Providence
   and hid in fear

Now I can see clearly the path ahead
Your hand in mine
   as I take the lead

I'm sorry that I doubted the Inner Voice
You've hidden deep in my soul

   Now I know better

I will listen and act without fear
I will move forward with confidence and hope

   Thanks for pointing the Way

A New Horizon

Your ways are not my ways, O Lord.

I would not have chosen these turns in the road.
But my eyes are affixed
    Looking straight ahead.

And my heart is filled with wonder.
    What is coming next?
    What doors will open?
    How will this all end?

As I gaze across the horizon
and make my way to a new place,
I sense Your presence—Real presence.

As far as I can see, Your grace is there.
As deep as I can go inside, Your healing touch is there.

Blessed are You, O Lord our God
Keeper of the New Horizon.

Amen.

After fifteen months of unemployment, I was out of shape, mentally and physically. My inner workaholic had learned how to "relax" and enjoy the moment. I hadn't had to use my brain as critically as before and I had gotten "soft."

Then it was time for my first work trip, the security regulations of air travel, the long lines I hated, and time "above the clouds."

As the plane taxied down the runway, I realized I had come full circle. When I looked out the window at the clouds below, tears welled up in my eyes. I recalled the moment my job ended, selling our home and moving cross country. I re-membered the humbling gift of staying with my cousins for fifteen months and the hard life lessons of my job hunt.

I savored my time with Margo and the "Chosen Family" we had created, an extended family based on our conscious choice to share life and faith. Now here I was, back on the road. The gratitude I felt was overwhelming. The presence of God I had felt throughout my unemployment was now unmistakable. I had been led to this place and I had chosen to respond in faith.

And then Bob died. We all do, but the timing of Bob's passing was like a trumpet call for me. It re-minded me to get busy living, because life is short and God is calling. Let it be a reminder for you as well. I pray for open doors in your life and that you find the perfect place to put your passion and strengths to work.

No trial has come to you but what is human. God is faithful and will not let you be tried beyond your strength; but with the trial he will also provide a way out, so that you may be able to bear it. (1 Corinthians 10:13)

For Reflection

1. Go back to your list of emotions from Chapter 1. Do you notice any difference? Make a new list. How do you feel now?

2. Who's been your biggest fan and cheerleader? How can you thank him or her? Do it!

3. What have you learned about God's presence and grace during your waiting?

4. What will you do to stay connected with your faith community?

EPILOGUE

Blessed be God forever

The prayers, reflections, and meditations contained here are part of my journey through the maze of unemployment. I prayed for fifteen months that I would find the "right" job. Each week I maintained a schedule of job searches, applications, and interviews while my wife, Margo, offered support and encouragement. Thank God she was working.

We spent more than a year living with my cousins, Carol and Ken, with everything we owned in storage. Their extra bedroom proved that we really needed very little to survive. Cooking meals together and raising a glass to toast "Blessed be God forever" became the best antidote to depression and self-pity I could have ever hoped to find.

I am a "cradle Catholic." I have been in parish, diocesan, and publishing ministry for most of my life. But I was not prepared for the simple power, elegance, and grace waiting to be found in the Sunday assembly of Saint Stephen's parish in Renton, Washington. Free from the former distractions of my work, I found comfort, peace, challenge, and the presence of Christ in every celebration of the Eucharist. Even though I was living on an unemployment check, I felt more rooted and connected than I had in many years. The honest admission of my limits made me grateful for the simple gift of life and reminded me that opportunities to serve don't stop even if you're unemployed.

Another blessing was participating in the CLO (Concerned Lifers Organization) of the Washington State Reformatory in Monroe, where we meet every Monday evening with the inmates.

As we sat in our circle, MY situation suddenly didn't matter. Thoughts of job hunting disappeared into a rhythm of introductions and story-telling. The khaki pants blur the reality that one man holds an MBA from a prestigious School of Business, one served as an Armed Services Commander, one had a thriving crack cocaine business, and another is clinically schizophrenic. The men of the CLO offer support, discuss inmate mental health, sentencing reform, and how to make things right beyond the laws that were broken. The proverb IS true: "The shortest distance between a human being and the truth IS a story." The tales of these men who are living "life without parole" taught me that nothing cages the human spirit. I learned all of this because I was willing to "check my ego" and volunteer. I invite you to do the same and step out of your comfort zone. Raise your hand and offer yourself to a local help agency or faith-based organization.

Thanks to a phone call from afar and an offer to put my passions and strengths to work, the next chapter in my story has begun. I have a wonderful position that I love, and I thank God every day for all the lessons I learned in my months of waiting and listening. God WILL make a way! He did for me. He will for you.

Here's to open doors in your life. Enjoy the following reminders as you wait and pray, live, and remember to breathe…

TIMOTHY MULLNER, DMIN

A TOP TEN LIST
FOR FINDING YOUR WAY
THROUGH UNEMPLOYMENT

1. **Check your pride at the door.** The person in line behind you may have been a billionaire who lost it all or has as much experience and as many degrees as you do. Learn to accept EVERY bit of help offered to you.

2. **Take Advantage of Every Local Work Center Training Session.** Use their computers for your job search. Think about what you've always wanted to do, then talk with people and find classes in that area of interest. Explore free job counseling or talk with a rabbi, priest, wise relative, or mentor for added support.

3. **Think Core Values, Skills, and Strengths.** Define what you do best. Tell people about your skills and passions. Write down the ten most important things that drive you. Now cut the list to five. These are your Core Values. What work best matches your Core Values?

4. **Embrace Your Emotions.** Wade into your sea of feelings with reflection, prayer, writing, and reading. TALK about how you feel being unemployed. Attend family gatherings and connect with a place of worship. Call a long-lost friend and tell him what's really going on in your life.

5. Get Creative. Engage in a creative process, such as cooking, painting, music, sewing, or woodworking. Go to art museums on their free day, explore your library, start a book club, find an activity that fills your soul.

6. Get Back to the Basics. Do what you need to do to survive, but avoid the temptation to cancel everything that's not essential. Save money by eating real food rather than processed food. Contact any creditors. Many will help you find payment solutions.

7. Volunteer. Stop the pity party and get out in the community. Volunteering can establish relationships with managers and build credibility when positions become available. Schools and churches need "person power" for kids and all kinds of projects. Offer your abilities to a non-profit. Spend time in a homeless shelter.

8. Have Fun. Take advantage of free events, church concerts, and community festivals. The simple joy of a family game night can restore a sense of connection and balance to your out-of-control life. Surround yourself with the beauty of local parks. Share potluck and neighborhood meals.

9. Stay Healthy. You are no good to anyone if you are DEAD. Pay attention to your blood pressure, weight gain, and don't miss your annual checkup. Explore stress-reduction exercises. Lower your caffeine and alcohol intake, and drink water, water, and more water. Walk or exercise a minimum of five times per week. Spend time outside!

10. Practice Gratitude. Be thankful for what you DO have and the important people in your life. A toast or simple blessing at mealtime helps to form a life of gratitude. Give thanks for three things before you go to sleep each night.

You are my servant;

I chose you, I have not rejected you—

Do not fear: I am with you;

Do not be anxious: I am your God.

ISAIAH 41:9–10